LIVING WITH ASTHMA

LIVING WITH ASTHMA

by Christine Zuchora-Walske

Content Consultant
Robin Evans-Agnew, RN, PhD, Assistant Professor,
Nursing and Healthcare Leadership
University of Washington Tacoma

LIVING WITH HEALTH CHALLENGES

CREDITS

Published by ABDO Publishing Company, PO Box 398166, Minneapolis, MN 55439. Copyright © 2014 by Abdo Consulting Group, Inc. International copyrights reserved in all countries. No part of this book may be reproduced in any form without written permission from the publisher. The Essential Library™ is a trademark and logo of ABDO Publishing Company.

Printed in the United States of America,
North Mankato, Minnesota
092013
012014

THIS BOOK CONTAINS AT LEAST 10% RECYCLED MATERIALS.

Editor: Jenna Gleisner
Series Designer: Becky Daum

Photo credits: Thinkstock, cover, 3, 19, 40, 52, 84, 88, 90, 96; Rick Becker-Leckrone/Shutterstock Images, 8; Alila Medical Media/Shutterstock Images, 14; Shutterstock Images, 16, 22, 33, 43, 68, 76; Dean Drobot/Shutterstock Images, 28; Andrew Zarivny/Shutterstock Images, 37; iStockphoto, 45; Purestock/Thinkstock, 49; Odua Images/Shutterstock Images, 58; Dragon Images/Shutterstock Images, 60; Digital Vision/Thinkstock, 62; Ebruchez/Wikimedia Commons, 67; Preto Perola/Shutterstock Images, 70; Olga Reutska/Shutterstock Images, 72; Lucky Business/Shutterstock Images, 79; Wavebreak Media/Thinkstock, 82; Shvaygert Ekaterina/Shutterstock Images, 92

Library of Congress Control Number: 2013945889

Cataloging-in-Publication Data

Zuchora-Walske, Christine.
 Living with asthma / Christine Zuchora-Walske.
  p. cm. -- (Living with health challenges)
Includes bibliographical references and index.
ISBN 978-1-62403-242-4
1. Asthma--Juvenile literature.   I. Title.
616.2--dc23

2013945889

CONTENTS

EXPERT ADVICE

I joined the faculty of the University of Washington in 2012. I have worked extensively with middle and high school teens throughout my career as an Outward Bound instructor, a middle and high school nurse, a public health nurse, and a program director at the American Lung Association. I have worked in asthma camps, taught teens and their parents about asthma control, helped schools design better programs for teens, and worked to change laws for tobacco and asthma in schools. In the last 15 years, I have been increasingly interested in helping teens with asthma—especially those from ethnic, racial, or sexual minorities—demand more from health care and society to make air cleaner, medications easier, and asthma care more equal for an eventual permanent end to the asthma epidemic.

The teenage years are especially important for asthma for both genders. Teens find they have to figure out a way to take control of asthma as they are learning to take care of themselves without their parents' help. Yet, teens don't get to make all the choices about how to keep a clean environment so their asthma doesn't flare up. Being a teen is very stressful, and that does not help in the control of asthma, especially if it has been a long time since the last attack. Teens with asthma often don't know who else has asthma and they feel alone, even though one out of every ten teens has asthma.

Contrary to popular belief, asthma doesn't make you weak: asthma is the most common chronic disease amongst Olympic athletes. Asthma is about how it is controlled. If you cough at night or use your inhaler more than twice a week (not just before exercise), then your asthma is most likely not under control.

But be hopeful: scientists are discovering that asthma is a collection of diseases, and new treatments are on the way. Scientists have clearly linked air pollution to asthma, and cities, towns, and states are beginning to clean up our air. There are plenty of other teens with asthma in your area. Get involved through your public health department, connect to other teens for support, and work together to clean up our environment.

— *Robin Evans-Agnew, RN, PhD, Assistant Professor, Nursing and Healthcare Leadership, University of Washington Tacoma*

1

WHAT IS ASTHMA?

Nora couldn't remember a time when she didn't feel congested. Sometimes she sneezed and coughed a lot—especially in the spring and fall. It was kind of a pain, but it wasn't that unusual. Nora had noticed a lot of her schoolmates had the same problem.

Living with asthma can make it difficult to enjoy the outdoors.

Seasonal allergies were pretty common where Nora lived.

One morning as Nora walked to school with her friend Will, she noticed the neighborhood looked and smelled wonderful after a long, snowy winter. The grass was green, the trees were finally leafing, and the crabapple blossoms were just about to open. It felt great to be outdoors. But as Nora walked along, she realized she was having trouble chatting with Will. She couldn't quite catch her breath. So she kept walking but stopped talking. By the time they reached school, Nora was feeling dizzy. She sat down on the school steps, gasping for breath.

Will immediately called out to Mr. King, the teacher monitoring the entrance, and together Mr. King and Will helped Nora to the nurse's office. Ms. McDougall, the nurse, helped Nora relax and rest. Twenty minutes later, Nora felt better, but she was confused about what had just happened. When Ms. McDougall came back to check on her, Nora asked, "What was that? I think my allergies got really bad and then I just got really dizzy." Ms. McDougall answered, "Nora, I think you may have just had an asthma attack." An *asthma attack*, Nora thought. Since when did she have asthma, and what did this all mean?

HOW HEALTHY LUNGS WORK

Asthma is a disease of the lungs that causes difficulty in breathing. To understand what happens when someone has an asthma attack, it's important to first understand how the respiratory system normally functions.

When you inhale and exhale, your lungs perform a gas exchange in which the lungs take in oxygen and push out carbon dioxide. While breathing, your lungs work together with the rest of your respiratory system. The four key parts of this system are the airways, the lungs, the blood vessels linked to the lungs, and the muscles that create the motion of breathing.

Breathing begins with your muscles. The key muscles that enable breathing are your diaphragm, the dome-shaped muscle beneath

OXYGEN IN, CARBON DIOXIDE OUT

Your body needs oxygen so your cells can convert food into energy in a process called metabolism. The main energy source for your cells comes from a chain reaction that uses oxygen. Oxygen and nutrients are in this chain reaction. Energy and carbon dioxide then come out. The carbon dioxide is a waste product. Your body must get rid of carbon dioxide because if too much of it builds up, it becomes a toxic acid. All your cells need a continuous supply of nutrients and oxygen in order to produce the energy that powers the body functions that keep you alive.

your lungs, and your intercostal muscles, which lie between your ribs.

At the beginning of each inhalation, your diaphragm contracts, or tightens. When it contracts, it flattens out a bit. The top of your diaphragm moves downward, and the edges move outward, expanding your rib cage and lungs. The intercostal muscles also help expand your rib cage and lungs. This expansion creates a vacuum inside your lungs, which sucks in air through your airways. Imagine an accordion sucking in air as you expand it. Inhaling works similarly to that.

Your airways are passages that carry air from the outside of your body to the inside of your body. First, air enters your body through your nose and mouth. Your nose and mouth warm and wet the air, which then travels downward through your trachea, the tube that leads from your nose and mouth to your lungs. At its lower end, your trachea branches into two tubes called bronchi. Each bronchus leads into your lungs, where it branches into many smaller airways called bronchioles. The bronchioles end in air sacs called alveoli. The alveoli look similar to bunches of tiny, round grapes.

Each alveolus is wrapped in a mesh of capillaries, which are linked to the larger network of vessels that move blood through your body. Oxygen moves from the air inside

CLEANUP CREW

Your airways keep the air you breathe clean in a few different ways. First, hairs in your nose and saliva in your mouth trap some particles and germs from the air. Second, a flap of tissue called the epiglottis covers your trachea when you swallow, keeping food and drink out of your airways. Third, your trachea, bronchi, and bronchioles are lined with white blood cells that help fight infection. They are also lined with tiny, mucus-coated hairs called cilia. The cilia trap more germs and particles and sweep them upward to your nose or mouth, where you either swallow them or cough and sneeze them out of your body.

the alveoli through their thin walls into the blood inside the capillaries. The oxygen-rich blood travels through the pulmonary vein to your heart, which then pumps it to the rest of your body.

Meanwhile, your pulmonary artery delivers deoxygenated, carbon dioxide–rich blood to the capillaries surrounding the alveoli. The carbon dioxide moves from the blood in the capillaries to the air in the alveoli. Then you exhale the carbon dioxide–rich air.

When you exhale, your diaphragm relaxes. The top of your diaphragm moves upward and the edges move inward, compressing your rib cage and lungs. The intercostal muscles also help compress your rib cage and lungs. This compression forces air out of your lungs, through your trachea, then out of your body through your nose or mouth.

WHAT HAPPENS IF YOU HAVE ASTHMA

If you have asthma, your bronchial tubes are in a constant, low-level state of inflammation. Inflammation is your immune system's response to illness, injury, pain, or stress. Blood, antibodies, and other immune substances rush in to break down damaged tissue, kill germs, and rebuild healthy tissue. This process may cause swelling, redness, heat, pain, loss of function, or any combination thereof. Short-term, or temporary inflammation, is beneficial because it is a necessary step toward healing. Long-term, or constant inflammation, however, can be dangerous for a variety of reasons, depending on the circumstances.

For asthma sufferers, inflammation is harmful because it makes your airways twitchy, or oversensitive. Your airways tend to react strongly to conditions or substances that have little or no effect on the airways of people without asthma, such as a strong smell, a blast of wind, pollen in the air, stress, exercise, or a certain food.

Your trachea, bronchi, and bronchioles all have walls ringed with muscle on the outside. On the inside, these airways are lined with mucus-producing cells. When your airways react

Pathology of Asthma

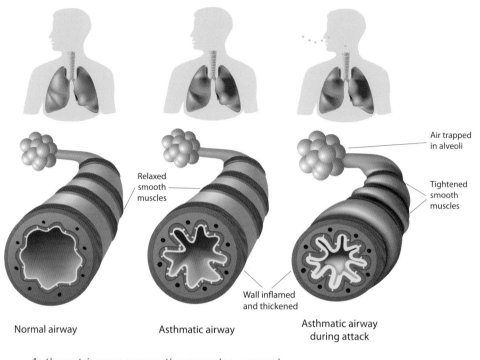

Relaxed smooth muscles

Air trapped in alveoli

Tightened smooth muscles

Wall inflamed and thickened

Normal airway

Asthmatic airway

Asthmatic airway during attack

Asthma triggers cause the muscles around your airways to tighten, constricting airflow.

to a condition or substance, the muscles around them tighten. This narrows your airways. The swelling of inflamed tissues can worsen, too, narrowing your airways even more. And your airway lining might make extra mucus. All of these reactions make it harder for air to flow in and out of your lungs.

In short: asthma is a chronic, or long-term, lung disease with a key characteristic of inflamed airways. This inflammation leads to physical reactions that narrow the airways. As a result, asthma causes recurrent bouts of wheezing, chest tightness, shortness of breath, and coughing. In 2011, 9.5 percent of children in the United States had been diagnosed with asthma. Among US adults, 8.2 percent had asthma.[1]

ASK YOURSELF THIS

- *Have you ever had trouble breathing while trying to accomplish simple activities, such as walking? Did you tell anyone?*

- *Have you ever gotten the wind knocked out of you; had a really bad respiratory infection, such as cold, flu, bronchitis, or pneumonia; or overexerted yourself and had trouble catching your breath? How did it feel?*

- *Have you ever experienced or witnessed an asthma attack? What happened?*

- *What if Nora were alone on her way to school as her asthma attack set in? How do you think the situation could have ended differently if Will were not there to help?*

2

ASTHMA SYMPTOMS

Fifteen-year-old Daniel recalled the fateful
day he was diagnosed with asthma. He
was 13 years old then. It was fall two
years ago, and he was out in the yard helping
his parents rake leaves. His parents raked them
into piles, and Daniel took it from there. He

Each case of asthma can consist of different symptoms; identifying your own will help you manage your asthma.

spread some on the flower beds and bagged up the rest.

One minute he was just fine. The next minute, he was struggling to breathe. He suddenly felt very sick and very scared. He had no idea what was happening to him.

His parents noticed that he'd stopped working. He was rooted to one spot, and he'd gone quiet. His eyes were wide with fright, and his mouth hung open as he wheezed. Daniel's dad ran inside and called 911 while his mom stayed with him.

It didn't take long for paramedics to arrive. They could tell what was happening right away. Daniel was having a severe asthma attack. On the way to the hospital, they gave him medications that helped ease his breathing a bit. Daniel stayed in the hospital overnight so he could recover fully and so doctors could have some time to observe him, learn more about his medical history, run tests, and make recommendations to his family doctor.

Daniel could remember how scared he felt. But he also realized how things had changed. Over the past two years, Daniel had learned a lot about asthma. In particular, he learned a lot about *his* asthma. He got really good at recognizing and responding to his unique symptoms. Daniel didn't panic anymore, and neither did his parents or friends.

FOUR KEY SYMPTOMS

The tricky part about defining asthma symptoms is their variability. If you have asthma, it's important that you understand the disease as well as you possibly can. You should not only get to know your asthma symptoms, but also get familiar with the full range of possibilities—and expect the unexpected.

The symptoms of asthma vary from person to person—in type, intensity, duration, and frequency. Symptoms can also vary from episode to episode. No specific set of symptoms or pattern of symptoms applies to every person with asthma or every asthma attack. When you're diagnosed with asthma, your doctor also grades its severity. Your grading shows your physical condition, lung function, and how frequent and severe your symptoms are. Your doctor will also grade the degree of satisfaction and control you feel you have over your asthma. This helps treat your specific case of asthma more effectively.

A few key symptoms do appear in most people with asthma at some point. These four common symptoms are wheezing, coughing, chest discomfort, and shortness of breath. Some adolescents also complain of stomachaches.

Coughing is your body's way of trying to clear your airways.

WHEEZING

Wheezing is the noise air makes when you breathe through narrowed airways. It can happen while you're inhaling, exhaling, or both. Wheezing usually sounds like high-pitched whistling, but some people with asthma say that when you're wheezing, it sounds like a cat purring inside your chest. Wheezing is a result of swelling, muscle tightening, or mucus in your airways.

If you're wheezing, you'll most likely know it. Even if you can't hear a whistling or purring sound with your ears, you'll feel the wheezing in your chest as a vibration, pressure, or some other type of discomfort. If your wheezing is mild or moderate, others might not be able to hear it. It should be audible through a stethoscope, though.

COUGHING

Coughing is a reflex to a blockage in your airways. You may experience a chronic cough without wheezing. In some people with asthma, chronic coughing is the main—or only—symptom. Coughing, like wheezing, can be caused by many different conditions. Asthma is one cause of chronic coughing. Some other causes are allergies, smoking, bronchitis, and emphysema. An asthma cough is recognizable by a few key traits: harshness, persistence, and timing.

The typical cough of asthma is harsh. It is deep, unproductive (doesn't bring up mucus), and can be so violent it makes you throw up. You might cough a half-dozen times without being able to catch your breath. An asthma cough is usually persistent, too. That doesn't mean you're coughing all the time. Rather, it means the cough never truly goes away. An asthma cough can last for months if you don't get it treated. Finally, an asthma cough has distinct timing. It's especially obvious or severe after exercising, after you breathe in cold air, or at night.

COUGH-VARIANT ASTHMA

Cough-variant asthma is a type of asthma in which chronic coughing is the main—and sometimes only—symptom. It is typically a dry, nonproductive cough without wheezing or shortness of breath. The coughing in cough-variant asthma often begins at night. Cough-variant asthma is especially common in young children. But it can occur in people of any age. Asthma is the cause of approximately 25 percent of all chronic coughs.[1]

CHEST DISCOMFORT

Another common symptom of asthma is chest discomfort. This discomfort may feel like pain, pressure, or tightness in your chest. Some people with asthma describe this sensation by saying it feels as if an elephant is sitting on your chest. Chest tightness often feels worse when you're lying down. That's because lying down can cause mucus to collect in your airways, decrease your lung volume, and increase the volume of blood in your lungs.

Dyspnea, a common symptom of asthma, can make physical activity extremely difficult.

People once believed the hard work of breathing that muscles must do during an asthma attack causes the sensation of chest tightness in asthma. But recent research shows this is probably not the case. Rather, the feeling of chest tightness more likely comes from nerve cells that are stimulated when airway muscles contract.

SHORTNESS OF BREATH

If you have shortness of breath, it means you're having a hard time breathing. Health professionals call this symptom dyspnea. Dyspnea has no strict medical definition. Some people with dyspnea say they can't catch their breath, can't take a deep enough breath, or can't get enough air. Some say they feel air-hungry. Others say they feel smothered or feel as if they're suffocating. People who can't pinpoint their symptom as shortness of breath may describe It as fatigue or inability to carry out ordinary activities.

Shortness of breath can also be a sign of several disorders, including asthma. In people with asthma, shortness of breath is often a sign of poor asthma control or worsening asthma. Dyspnea due to asthma is caused by a combination of airway constriction, intense muscle effort, and disturbed signals between the respiratory nerve cells and respiratory muscles.

EARLY WARNING SIGNS

One of the best ways to protect your health is learning to recognize asthma's early warning signs. These signs are physical changes that may happen right before an attack or at its very beginning. These changes may include a change in your lung function as measured on a peak-flow meter.

You may develop cold- or allergy-like symptoms, such as congestion, cough, headache, runny nose, sneezing, or sore throat. Shortness of breath, exhaustion, weakness, wheezing, or coughing could be experienced during or after exercise. You might also notice a change in your attitude; for example, it's natural to feel irritable and cranky as a result of fatigue and sleeplessness.

PEAK-FLOW METER

A peak-flow meter is a handheld device that measures how quickly you can blow air out of your lungs. It is portable and simple to use, unlike the larger and more complex spirometer typically used in health-care settings. A peak-flow meter is a key tool for monitoring asthma by yourself. If you have moderate or severe asthma, a history of severe attacks, or if you have trouble recognizing warning signs, your doctor may prescribe the use of a peak-flow meter.

You simply blow into the meter as hard as you can three times and take your best reading. The reading gives clues about the condition of your airways. When your peak-flow readings drop lower than usual, it's a sign your airways are narrowing.

Usually early warning signs are mild. They don't stop you from going about your everyday routine. But they're important to recognize because they can help you prevent an asthma attack or keep it from worsening.

OTHER SYMPTOMS OF AN ASTHMA ATTACK

If you have asthma, another important step you can take to protect your health is knowing the many symptoms of an asthma attack in addition to the four key symptoms.

You may have difficulty carrying out everyday activities, talking, or exercising. You might feel distracted or exhausted. You may find yourself breathing rapidly, sighing, or sweating. Others might remark on your paleness. Your lips or fingernails may take on a bluish or grayish hue caused by a lack of oxygen in your blood. All of these symptoms could result from insufficient oxygen intake.

If you have been wheezing and the wheezing stops suddenly but you are not able to breathe any better, you are experiencing silent chest. Silent chest is not very common, but it means that your condition is worsening and you're not breathing well enough to wheeze. Anxiety or panic may occur when you're having trouble getting enough air. You may notice a

CYANOSIS

Cyanosis is a blue or gray discoloration of your lips or the skin underneath your fingernails. It's caused by a lack of oxygen in your blood. Your red blood cells bring oxygen to your body's tissues. Most of the time, these blood cells carry a full supply of oxygen and are bright red, giving your skin a pinkish or reddish color. Blood that has lost its oxygen has a dark color and is more bluish red. So when your blood is low in oxygen, your skin turns bluish. Because all the body's cells need oxygen, tissue damage can occur if low oxygen goes on too long. Cyanosis is a sign of an asthma attack that needs immediate medical attention.

sense of unease before you notice you're not breathing well. And for some people, anxiety itself can trigger asthma flare-ups. Once you know what symptoms to watch for, you'll know when to act.

ASK YOURSELF THIS

- *If you or someone you know has asthma, what are his or her symptoms?*

- *Why do you think it's important to understand and recognize all the symptoms of asthma?*

- *You may have noticed while reading this chapter that asthma symptoms often occur or get worse at night. How might that make asthma more difficult to cope with?*

- *How might the various asthma symptoms make life difficult for someone with asthma?*

- *Have you ever had symptoms similar to Daniel's? What did you do?*

3

THE CAUSES OF ASTHMA

Sheena was 17 years old. She lived in Los Angeles, California. She liked a lot of things about living in L.A. She loved having both the ocean and the mountains nearby. She loved all the excitement.

Checking the air quality index (AQI) in your area each day is an easy way to help manage your asthma.

But Sheena did not love the air pollution in L.A. Her hometown was famous for its smoggy, dirty air. It wasn't bad all the time—and Sheena's dad said it was much better than it had been 40 years ago when he'd grown up. But the air wasn't that great, either. L.A. had a lot of auto traffic and industry; it sat in a warm, mountain-ringed valley; and it didn't usually have strong winds. So on many days of the year, the air got dirty and stayed that way. L.A. constantly made the list of US cities with the most polluted air.

Air pollution was hard on everyone in L.A. It caused a lot of coughing, burning eyes, and sore throats. But it was especially hard on Sheena because of her asthma. Sheena knew smog, soot, and vehicle exhaust were powerful asthma triggers. So every day before she went outside, she checked the air quality index (AQI) on her phone.

This morning, as Sheena woke up for school, she noticed how nice it already was outside—a great morning to walk to school, she thought. She headed down to the kitchen for breakfast.

"Walking today?" asked her dad as he poured himself a bowl of cereal.

"Hope so! I haven't checked the AQI yet, though," Sheena responded. She pulled out her smartphone to bring up her AQI app. The map showed the color orange over the L.A. area, meaning outdoor exercise wasn't a healthy choice for her today.

"Ugh, will I ever be able to walk to school without risking an asthma attack? Do you have time to give me a ride instead?"

WHAT CAUSES ASTHMA?

Asthma is related to allergy. Both are disorders of the immune system—your body's system for defending against potentially harmful invaders—and they often appear together. Both asthma attacks and allergic reactions occur when the body overreacts to perceived—but not actual—dangers.

Nobody knows exactly what causes asthma, but scientists think asthma is due to a combination of genetic and environmental factors. When these factors meet, usually in childhood, a person may develop asthma. In other words, the capacity to have asthma is genetic. But even if you are born with the genetic capacity to have asthma, you will not automatically have asthma symptoms. You must have the genes that predispose you to asthma, and you must be exposed to triggers to which you are genetically programmed to respond, as well as irritants that aggravate your immune system.

Researchers have found that certain traits make it more likely a person will develop asthma. Factors that contribute to asthma development are atopy, or inherited allergies; having parents with asthma; having certain respiratory infections as a child; and exposure to certain allergens, irritants, and viruses in early childhood while the immune system is still developing.

THE HYGIENE HYPOTHESIS

In recent decades, the rates of allergy and asthma have skyrocketed in Western nations, such as those in North America and Europe. Scientists once believed this was happening because of increasing air pollution. A group of researchers investigated this idea in 1999. They studied allergy and asthma rates in western and eastern Germany, which had been separate nations since 1949 but had just reunified in 1990. Western Germany was cleaner, more modern, and more prosperous. Eastern Germany was poorer and dirtier.

The scientists expected to find higher allergy and asthma rates in eastern Germany. But the rates were actually higher in western Germany. This finding led the researchers to develop the hygiene hypothesis. The hypothesis proposes that children who are around many other children, animals, and germs early in life develop more tolerance for the irritants that cause allergies and asthma. When children live an overly sanitary lifestyle, their immune systems overreact to harmless substances such as allergens, irritants, and other asthma triggers.[1]

WHAT TRIGGERS THE SYMPTOMS OF AN ASTHMA ATTACK?

An asthma attack happens when you come into contact with a trigger. An asthma trigger is a condition or substance that causes asthma symptoms to either start or get worse. Just as people have different asthma symptoms, they also have different triggers. Outdoor air pollution, such as that experienced by Sheena in the story at the beginning of this chapter, is one common trigger. It falls into a category of triggers called irritants. The other categories are allergens, medications, emotional behaviors, exercise, infections, and weather.

ALLERGENS

An allergen is any substance that causes an allergic reaction. An allergic reaction is an exaggerated immune system response to something that does not bother most people. This physical response may include runny nose, sneezing, itching, rash, swelling, or asthma.

An allergen can be nearly anything, but some allergens are more common than others. Common allergens include pollen, dust mites, cockroaches, mold spores, pet dander, foods and food additives, insect stings, and drugs. Any of these allergens is a possible asthma trigger.

If you are a pet lover with asthma, talk to your physician about ways to keep your pet around while still managing your asthma.

Dust mites—bugs too tiny to see—live in mattresses, pillows, bedding, carpet, upholstered furniture, clothes, stuffed toys, and other fabric items. They eat the dead skin cells people shed. Their droppings and parts from their dead bodies can trigger asthma in people who are allergic to dust mites.

MEDICATIONS

Medications can be allergens, so they can trigger asthma attacks by causing allergic reactions. But even in people without drug allergies, drugs can be asthma triggers. Two types of medications are common asthma triggers. Beta blockers, for example, make your heart beat slower and less forcefully, which reduces your blood pressure and helps your blood vessels open up to improve blood flow. Beta blockers also block dilation (widening) of your airways. That's why they're dangerous if you have asthma.

Another group of drugs that often triggers asthma are nonsteroidal anti-inflammatory drugs (NSAIDs). NSAIDs are a class of medicines that do not contain hormonal substances called steroids. Some of the most common NSAIDs that can trigger asthma are aspirin, ibuprofen, ketoprofen, and naproxen. People usually take these drugs to relieve pain or reduce fever. But up to one-fifth of people with asthma can't take certain NSAIDs because they are triggers.[2] Although they reduce inflammation, which would seem to help asthma, they also hinder an enzyme called cyclooxygenase-1, which in turn brings on asthma symptoms.

EMOTIONS AND EXERCISE

Emotions themselves can't trigger asthma, but they can lead to behaviors that trigger asthma. For example, sadness can cause crying. Happiness may cause laughter. Anger may cause yelling. Fear may cause screaming, jumping, running, or other panicky actions. Teens suffering from hardships at home or bullying may experience chronic stress. All these behaviors involve deep, rapid breathing. Exercise causes deep, rapid breathing, too. That's why exercise is another common asthma trigger. So what's the problem with deep, rapid breathing? One would think large doses of oxygen should be good for a person with a breathing disorder.

ASTHMA AND INFLUENZA

If you have asthma, you're no more likely to get influenza, or flu, than anyone else. But flu could be a big problem for you. You already have inflammation in your airways, and flu can cause even more inflammation. When a flu virus gets into your lungs, it can trigger asthma, make symptoms worse, and lead to serious diseases such as pneumonia. If you have asthma and catch flu, you are more likely than others to end up in the hospital.

But large doses of oxygen may in fact be the problem. According to Dr. Konstantin Buteyko and practitioners of the Buteyko method, breathing too quickly and too deeply lowers the level of carbon dioxide in the blood so much that the airways constrict to conserve carbon dioxide and maintain the proper balance of oxygen and carbon dioxide.[3]

Another reason deep, rapid breathing is problematic for someone with asthma is because it brings a large amount of dry, cool air into the lungs. When you breathe in a normal, relaxed manner, you're usually breathing through your nose and breathing slow, relatively shallow breaths. When that air reaches your lungs, it's very warm and humid. In contrast, when you breathe deep and quickly, you're usually breathing through your mouth. Your mouth does not warm and wet the air as effectively as your nose does. This contrast between the cooler, drier incoming air and the warmer, wetter air already in your lungs can trigger an asthma attack.

INFECTIONS

Many people with asthma notice that ordinary illnesses trigger their asthma symptoms. This is particularly true for viral respiratory infections, such as the common cold and influenza.

For some people, an asthma attack is the first sign of illness. That's because when a virus invades airways, it develops for a day or two before it causes any symptoms. But the airways may react to the virus with an asthma attack even before the virus's symptoms appear.

IN THE AIR AND WEATHER

Some substances you inhale aren't actually allergens but can act similarly to them. These substances are called irritants. Irritants include

*Smog and other air pollutants can
trigger asthma symptoms.*

outdoor air pollution, tobacco smoke, smoke
from burning wood or grass, perfume, aerosol
sprays, chalk dust, paint fumes, and any

substances with strong odors. They may not only irritate your airways, but they may also trigger asthma attacks.

For many people with asthma, certain weather conditions may trigger asthma. This may be due to the atmospheric conditions themselves or the way the weather affects other potential triggers. For example, a blast of cold, dry winter air in the lungs may itself set off an asthma attack. Or a windy day may stir up allergens such as pollen, which then trigger asthma symptoms.

AQI

The air quality index (AQI) is a measure of five major air pollutants: ground-level ozone, particle pollution, carbon monoxide, sulfur dioxide, and nitrogen dioxide. The US Environmental Protection Agency (EPA) supplies this measurement. The measurements run from 0 to 500. The higher the number, the greater the level of air pollution and the greater the health concern. AQI numbers below 100 are considered satisfactory. AQI numbers above 100 are considered unhealthy. AQI is also divided into six color-coded categories to help you understand how air quality can affect your health.[4]

ASK YOURSELF THIS

- Do you live in or have you visited a city with poor air quality? If so, how did it affect your eyes, nose, lungs, or other parts of your body?

- Have you or has someone you know ever had a cold develop into a more serious condition? What happened?

- Do you have any allergies—and if so, what are they? Do you have asthma—and if so, what are your triggers? If you have both, are your allergens and asthma triggers related?

- Do you smoke tobacco or are you often around others who do? How do you notice its effects on your asthma?

WHO'S AT RISK FOR ASTHMA?

Sixteen-year-old James couldn't remember his first asthma attack. His mom told him it happened when he was a baby. It took James's family a few years to figure out his triggers. The main problem, it seemed, was stress.

Learning to manage your asthma symptoms can save you from attacks and keep you in the game.

As he got older, James began learning how to manage his feelings without having intense emotional outbursts. Just the other day, in fact, James had to practice calming himself down when the umpire at his baseball game made what James thought was a bad call. James was sure he'd slid into home base before the catcher tagged him with the ball.

The umpire yelled, "Out!"

James could feel a surge of adrenaline, and his heart began pounding. He started toward the umpire and took a deep breath, preparing to argue. The breath snapped him out of it. He knew what would happen if he started that argument. Getting thrown out of the game would be the least of it. The worst of it would likely be an asthma attack.

So James stopped himself. He whispered, "One. Two. Three. Four. Five. . . " By the time he got to ten, his anger had subsided, his heart stopped thumping, and he was able to walk away.

Once James learned to calm himself down, his asthma was well under control. In fact, he couldn't recall ever having had a really bad attack. He needed to take medication regularly. He also had to carry emergency medicine to inhale, just in case. But he rarely needed to use it.

Now in high school, he lived a completely normal teenage life. He goofed around with his friends, played baseball on his school's team, took classes that both challenged and bored him, and experienced all the ups and downs that other 16-year-olds did—all without landing in the hospital emergency room.

RISK FACTORS

Just as asthma takes many different forms in different people, it also has many different risk factors. Some are genetic, while others are environmental. Scientists agree the risk factors for all forms of asthma include both genes and the environment. Whether asthma develops depends on how these factors interact with one another.

Understanding the risk factors for asthma is an important tool for managing this condition. Some environmental risk factors are controllable. By minimizing these controllable factors, you or your parents can lower your risk of developing asthma. Of course, genetic risk factors are not controllable. So it's not possible to prevent asthma completely. But even if you have some risk factors you can't control, knowing about them can help you be on the

Research has proven that teenage girls are more susceptible to asthma than teenage boys.

lookout for symptoms. Recognizing and treating your asthma early can improve your prognosis.

GENETIC FACTORS

Among preadolescent children, more boys have asthma than girls—and more severely. Somewhere between the ages of 12 and 14, the situation reverses. Among adolescents and young adults, more females have asthma than males. Young women also tend to have more

WHAT ARE GENES?

All traits in living things, including susceptibility to asthma, depend upon genes. Genes are bits of the chemical code living things contain. This chemical code tells cells–the building blocks of all living things–how to make proteins. Proteins are responsible for carrying out cellular activities. Each protein is coded by a particular gene. Each trait depends on a particular combination of genes.

severe asthma than young men.[1] Some researchers suggest possible explanations for this switch around the age of puberty include hormonal changes and gender-specific differences in environmental exposures.[2]

A wide variety of studies on families and twins suggest the genes you inherit from your parents play an important role in whether you develop asthma or allergies. In fact, researchers have identified more than 100 individual genes related to allergies and asthma.[3]

Scientists are still trying to put together the pieces of asthma's genetic puzzle. Their research suggests the genes involved in asthma are ones that deal with threat or damage from the external environment, ones that modify mucus production, ones that modify allergic triggers at the cellular level, and ones that

Researchers have conducted studies on twins to investigate the links between genes and asthma.

help the immune system recognize invading microbes.

Having another allergic condition, such as eczema or hay fever, also raises your risk of developing asthma. Researchers have found that allergies to dust mites, cat dander, and cockroaches, in particular, are strongly associated with asthma. Many experts believe modern construction methods worsen this problem. These methods tend to seal up houses tightly in order to make them more energy-efficient. But such methods also reduce fresh air ventilation and increase exposure to indoor allergens.

Studies show high blood levels of the immunoglobulin E (IgE) antibody, an indicator of allergy, are also associated with asthma. IgE binds to allergens and triggers cells to release

THE COCKROACH FACTOR

In East Harlem, a neighborhood of New York City, 19 percent of five-year-olds have asthma. In the neighborhood next door, the Upper East Side, only 6 percent of five-year-olds have asthma.[4] Why is there such a big difference within such a small area? The answer: cockroaches. Cockroaches are common in East Harlem, where buildings are more densely packed with people, providing more food for the pesky insects. Cockroach saliva, droppings, and body parts are powerful allergens. They are a common cause for both allergic reactions and asthma.

Living in an area with high air pollution increases the cockroach effect. A study published in the *Journal of Allergy and Clinical Immunology* found that exposure to a type of pollution found in diesel exhaust and cheap home heating oil—both of which are plentiful in New York City—raises the risk of developing a cockroach allergy and related asthma.[5]

substances that cause inflammation. When this happens, allergic reactions—including asthma—can begin.

ENVIRONMENTAL FACTORS

The prevalence of asthma has increased markedly in recent decades. At the same time, our global environment has undergone rapid change. Scientists believe environmental changes, including changes in the way people behave, play a large role in the current asthma epidemic. There are several key environmental factors that increase your risk of developing asthma.

IGE TESTING

An IgE test measures the level of the IgE antibody in your blood. Antibodies are proteins made by your immune system that attack antigens. Antigens are substances foreign to your body, such as bacteria, viruses, and allergens. You have IgE antibodies in your blood, lungs, skin, and mucous membranes. High levels of IgE antibodies usually indicate either an allergic reaction or an infection by a parasite.

Certain behaviors by a pregnant mother can change the environment in her womb in a way that affects her baby's risk of developing asthma. Some behaviors raise the risk, while others lower it. For example, if your mother smoked while pregnant, that behavior negatively affected the environment in which you developed before birth. Studies have shown a strong, consistent link between prenatal smoking and children who wheeze. Smoking while pregnant also increases the baby's risk of food allergies. Similarly, research shows that if a mother takes antibiotics while pregnant, the child has a higher risk of developing asthma at a young age.

A pregnant mother's diet, by contrast, can actually help lower her child's risk of developing asthma. A variety of studies have examined the effects of foods with anti-inflammatory properties. This research has found that higher intakes of fish, fish oil, vitamin E, and zinc reduce the risk of wheezing in young children.[6]

There's a large body of evidence showing that exposure to tobacco smoke after birth is also damaging. If you live in an environment that contains secondhand smoke, you have a high risk of developing asthma and of worsening existing asthma. If you yourself smoke, you raise your risk even more.

Plenty of evidence exists showing that air pollution, both outdoors and indoors, is a key trigger for asthma attacks. It's not as clear what role air pollution plays in the initial development of asthma. Scientists think it is likely air pollution combines with genetic susceptibility and other factors to cause asthma.

In addition to its many negative impacts on health, smoking also worsens asthma.

Some research shows that children living in areas with high ozone levels and those in areas with a lot of traffic exhaust are more likely to develop asthma.[7] Adults who work in settings with high levels of dust, fumes, or other air pollutants also have a greater risk of developing asthma. Such occupations include farming, hairdressing, manufacturing, painting, cleaning, health care, and baking.[8]

Some studies show asthma is more common in overweight adults and children. There also seems to be more cases of uncontrolled asthma, as well as more days on medications, in overweight people with asthma. A 2013 study suggests leptin, a protein made by fat cells that plays a key role in energy metabolism, also regulates the diameter of airways.[9] This discovery could explain why obese people are prone to asthma.

ASTHMA RATE ON THE RISE

The number of people diagnosed with asthma in the United States increased by 4.3 million between 2001 and 2009, according to the US Centers for Disease Control and Prevention (CDC). In 2009, nearly one in 12 Americans had been diagnosed with asthma. Asthma costs increased from approximately $53 billion in 2002 to approximately $56 billion in 2007—approximately a 6 percent increase.[10]

ASK YOURSELF THIS

- *How many females and males do you know with asthma? Do you notice a trend?*

- *How many of your family members have asthma, if any? Does it seem to run in your family?*

- *Have you been surrounded by secondhand smoke, or do you smoke? Do you think it has contributed to your asthma?*

- *Although scientists have theories about the cause of the US asthma epidemic, no one knows for sure why it's happening. Why do you think asthma rates are on the rise?*

- *How many of the risk factors described in this chapter do you have?*

GETTING AN ASTHMA DIAGNOSIS

S ophie was 13 years old. She'd never been very successful in playing sports. She actually liked athletics, and she tried hard. But she just couldn't keep up.

Sophie ran out of energy quickly. In fact, she never felt completely well. She always

Being diagnosed with asthma can be scary, but it's the first step toward managing your asthma.

seemed to have some sort of cough or cold. She followed her health-care provider's advice to drink fluids, rest, and take medications for her congestion and coughing. But none of this really helped.

Finally, Sophie got fed up with feeling bad all the time. She asked her parents if she could see a different health-care provider. She hoped someone new could spot something in her constant symptoms besides a never-ending cold. So Sophie's parents took her to see a specialist. Dr. Meyer spent a lot of time with Sophie.

Dr. Meyer asked dozens of questions. Did anyone in Sophie's family have allergies? What typically happened when Sophie got sick? What were her symptoms? How long did they last? What helped? What didn't help? Where did she live? Where did she go to school? What activities did she participate in? Did she have any pets? And on and on.

Then Dr. Meyer examined Sophie. She checked Sophie's nose and throat. She listened to Sophie's lungs with a stethoscope. She examined Sophie's skin. She also ordered several tests, including a blood test, a skin test, and a few different types of breathing tests.

A few days later, Dr. Meyer called Sophie's parents. The verdict? Sophie had asthma. Although she'd never had an attack, her airways were chronically swollen. That was why Sophie coughed so much and always felt so tired. And allergies were to blame for her congestion. Sophie was allergic to the family cat. Dr. Meyer said the allergy was probably aggravating the asthma.

Sophie wasn't pleased to be diagnosed with asthma and a cat allergy. But at least now she knew what was wrong. And that meant she could do something about it.

SOLVING THE PUZZLE

Figuring out whether you have asthma can be tricky, and it can take a while. That's because each person with asthma has different symptoms.

If your regular health-care provider thinks you have asthma, he or she might send you to a specialist to help confirm that suspicion. Doctors who specialize in diagnosing and treating asthma include allergists, immunologists, and pulmonologists (allergy, immune system, and lung specialists, respectively). Any of these doctors will follow the same basic steps to diagnose asthma.

The first thing your doctor will most likely do is ask you questions about your family, your symptoms, your medical history, and your overall health. You might feel as if you're being interrogated, but try to be patient. Your doctor is gathering details that may provide clues as to whether asthma—or something else—is causing your symptoms. Your doctor may ask you to detail your symptoms, such as define what triggers them, their severity, and when they occur.

He or she will also ask you about your lifestyle. Whether or not you're often surrounded by pet dander, smoke, dust, and other irritants or if you have allergies can reveal important information for your doctor.

Next, your doctor will do a physical exam. Your doctor may examine your nose, throat, and upper airways. He or she might use a stethoscope to listen to your breathing. He or

BIRD FANCIER'S LUNG

Any pet that is warm-blooded can produce allergens that trigger asthma. But in some people, exposure to birds can cause asthma-like symptoms that aren't actually asthma. This condition is called bird fancier's lung. Its more formal name is allergic alveolitis or hypersensitivity pneumonitis. It is an inflammation of the alveoli. It causes breathlessness, tiredness, and sometimes weight loss. The main culprit is the bloom on the feathers of pet birds. Bloom is a substance that keeps the feathers sliding smoothly over one another. The bird spreads the substance over its feathers with its beak. It comes from the preen gland under the base of the bird's tail. Another trigger for asthma is the bird's droppings.

SPIROMETRY

Spirometry is a lung function test that's more sensitive and less portable than a peak-flow meter. A nurse or technician places a clip on your nose to keep your nostrils closed. You take a deep breath in, then breathe out as steadily as you can for several seconds into a tube that's attached to a machine called a spirometer. To ensure accuracy and consistency in your results, you will be asked to do this at least three times.

she will be on the lookout for wheezing, especially. And your doctor may examine your skin for signs of allergic reactions, such as eczema or hives. Finally, your doctor will perform one or more of the following diagnostic tests:

• Lung function test: A test called spirometry measures the volume of air you can breathe in and out. It also measures how quickly you can blow out air. After spirometry, your doctor may give you medicine and then retest you to see whether your results improve. Your doctor will most likely diagnose asthma if your initial test results are lower than normal but your results improve with medicine, and if your asthma has run in your family.

• Allergy test: Your doctor may use a blood test, a scratch test, or an intradermal test to find out which, if any, allergens affect you. A blood test can measure the amount of eosinophils or IgE in your blood. Scratch tests and intradermal tests both check for skin reactions to allergens.

- Bronchoprovocation: This test measures how sensitive your airways are. The doctor uses spirometry to measure your lung function during physical activity or after you inhale cold air or a special chemical called methacholine.

- Other tests: Your doctor may also perform other tests to rule out conditions that sometimes mimic asthma. For example, you may have to perform a sweat test to rule out cystic fibrosis, a genetic disease that affects breathing and digestion.

DIAGNOSING AND GRADING ASTHMA

If your doctor diagnoses you with asthma, he or she will also grade its severity. Asthma grading indicates your physical condition, lung function, and the frequency and severity of your symptoms. Grading helps your doctor choose the right treatment to keep your asthma in check.

ALLERGY SKIN TESTS

In a scratch test, drops of allergen extracts such as pollens, dust mites, molds, animal danders, or foods are allowed to enter scratches in your skin. A scratch test is painless and easy. It is less sensitive than an intradermal test and less likely to cause a severe reaction in a highly allergic person. In an intradermal test, allergen extracts are injected under the skin. Intradermal tests are very sensitive but can sometimes show false positive reactions. For people with severe allergies, intradermal tests may be more dangerous than scratch tests.

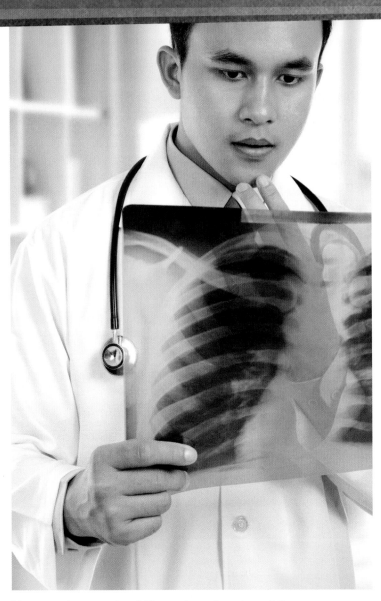

You may have a chest X-ray done to rule out the chance you have pneumonia or a foreign object stuck in your airways before being diagnosed with asthma.

Intermittent, or occasional, asthma is often defined by daytime wheezing and coughing on no more than two days per week and nighttime symptoms no more than twice per month.

Other than these episodes, there are no symptoms. If symptoms happen more often, you might have persistent asthma. Persistent asthma has three grades of severity.

The first grade of persistent asthma is mild persistent asthma. If you have mild persistent asthma, you experience daytime symptoms more than twice per week but less than once per day. Your symptoms may affect your activity level. You have nighttime symptoms more than twice per month but less than once per week. Without treatment, your lungs function at 80 percent or greater of normal lung function.[1]

The next grade is moderate persistent asthma. If you have moderate persistent asthma, you experience daytime symptoms every day. Your symptoms might disrupt your normal activities and make it hard to sleep. You have nighttime symptoms more than once per week. Without treatment, your lungs function at approximately 60 to 80 percent of normal lung function.[2]

BRITTLE ASTHMA

Brittle asthma is a rare form of severe asthma. People who have brittle asthma have the same symptoms as other people with asthma, but the symptoms are much harsher and come on suddenly and unpredictably. Brittle asthma is often resistant to traditional medication regimens and requires higher doses of medication.

Mild, moderate, and severe persistent asthma can all affect the way you exercise.

Sufferers of severe persistent asthma experience daytime symptoms often every day. Symptoms often disrupt normal activities and sleep. Without treatment, lungs function at less than 60 percent of normal lung function at this stage.[3]

ASK YOURSELF THIS

- *Have you ever had an allergy skin test? If so, what did it feel like? Did it show any allergic reactions? To what?*

- *If you found out you were allergic to a family pet, what would you do?*

- *Have you ever had spirometry? If so, what did your result show?*

- *Do you or someone you know have diagnosed intermittent or mild asthma? How does intermittent or mild asthma affect one's lifestyle?*

- *Do you know anyone with diagnosed moderate or severe asthma? If so, how does asthma affect this person's everyday life?*

- *Do you feel as if your asthma is under control? Have your symptoms worsened over time?*

TREATING ASTHMA AND PREVENTING ATTACKS

G raduation was just months away, and Isaac was planning for his freshman year of college. He knew college would be a big change, but he also knew he was different: Isaac had asthma. He'd had it since he was four years old. It was pretty awful at first. But now

Be proactive. Write to officials in your community to see what can be done to help fight pollution in your area.

it was well under control; Isaac hadn't had a bad attack for many years. And when he really thought hard about why he was in good health, Isaac realized his family was a key reason.

Isaac's asthma was triggered mainly by exposure to allergens. For him, the big culprits were dust mites and mold. His family did a lot to help him control his environment. They took special care with cleaning and ventilation to keep the house as free of dust and mold as possible. They also helped Isaac monitor his symptoms and remember his medications. But they wouldn't be living with him in the college dorms.

Isaac knew it might be easier to control his environment if he decided to live at home instead of signing up for a dorm room. Trying to avoid dust and mold in a crowded dorm full of college students would be challenging.

But Isaac was up to the challenge. He was determined to not let his asthma keep him from becoming independent. He wanted to live on campus. He wouldn't have to commute to campus, he knew it would be easier to make new friendships, and he'd be able to participate more in campus life. Isaac's parents agreed living in a dormitory would be okay. Soon Isaac learned he was paired with a roommate who also had asthma—and was just as concerned about keeping the room clean as Isaac was.

MEDICATIONS

No two people with asthma have the exact same medical needs. The right medical treatment for you depends on your triggers, your symptoms, your age, and what has or hasn't worked for you in the past.

Long-term control medications for asthma reduce inflammation in your airways or reduce your immune response to allergens. This, in turn, reduces the likelihood you'll have an asthma attack. Long-term control medications are usually taken daily.

BEFORE MODERN ASTHMA MEDICATION

Before scientists recognized asthma as an inflammatory disease and developed modern asthma medication, people with asthma tried many different treatments:

- An ancient Egyptian remedy was to heat a mixture of herbs on bricks and inhale their fumes.
- The ancient Greek physician Galen (130–200 CE) attempted to treat asthma by adding owl's blood to his wine.
- Moses Maimonides (1135–1204 CE), a rabbi, philosopher, and physician who lived in Spain, Morocco, and Egypt, recommended people with asthma avoid strong medication and get plenty of sleep, fluids, and chicken soup.
- Until the 1900s, a person in China with asthma inhaled a preparation of herbs containing ephedrine, a chemical that acts as a decongestant and relaxes the airways.[1]

Inhaled corticosteroids are artificial versions of hormones produced by your adrenal glands near the kidneys. They are powerful anti-inflammatory medicines. Leukotriene modifiers are oral drugs usually taken in pill form. They reduce the effects of leukotrienes, inflammatory chemicals made by the body. They help alleviate asthma symptoms for up to 24 hours. Side effects are rare but may include agitation, aggression, depression, hallucinations, or suicidal thoughts.

Long-acting beta agonists are inhaled medications that relax the airway muscles. They are used in combination with anti-inflammatory drugs, and deaths have occurred when long-acting beta agonists have been used alone. Rarely, long-acting beta agonists can interfere with quick-relief medications needed to quickly open airways or increase the risk of a severe asthma attack.

Theophylline is a daily pill that relaxes the airway muscles. It is not as common as it once was because it requires careful monitoring for side effects, and other drugs often work as well or better. People with allergy-related asthma can take allergy drugs to reduce their symptoms. These might include allergy shots, which gradually desensitize the immune system to specific allergens; omalizumab, an injected antibody specifically intended for allergic people with asthma, which also desensitizes the immune system; or decongestants and antihistamines. Antihistamines are drugs that block cell receptors for histamines. Histamines are compounds released by your immune system during an allergic reaction.

Sometimes people with asthma need fast-acting drugs to halt an asthma attack. Quick-relief medications quickly open swollen or constricted airways. There are three main types of quick-relief medications for asthma: short-acting beta agonists, ipratropium bromide, and systemic corticosteroids.

Short-acting beta agonists are inhaled drugs that relax airway muscles within minutes. They're meant to quickly relieve symptoms during an asthma attack. Ipratropium bromide is also an inhaled drug that immediately relaxes airway muscles. It's usually used for other respiratory diseases, but sometimes people with asthma take it when short-acting beta agonists aren't working. Systemic corticosteroids are drugs patients either take in pill form or inject intravenously. They relieve airway inflammation. Using them for a long time can harm skin, bones, and growth, so they're meant only for short-term use to treat severe asthma symptoms.

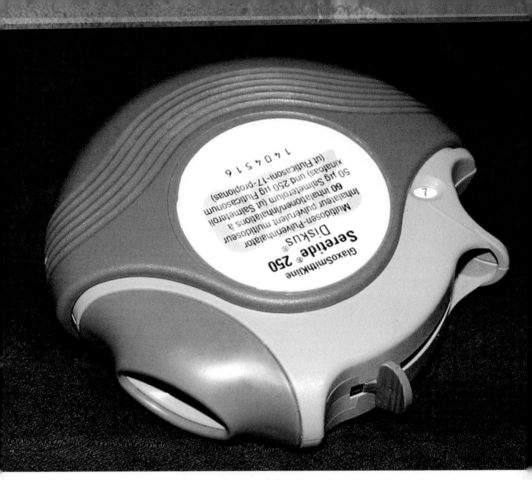

Combo inhalers, often used for daily asthma control, deliver a combination of corticosteroids and long-acting beta agonists in a fine dry powder form.

ALTERNATIVE TREATMENTS

Some people choose to treat their asthma with alternative therapies. Most people who choose these treatments use them in addition to—not in place of—medical treatment. If you use an alternative therapy, it's important to coordinate your care among your practitioners because all treatments can affect other treatments. Some

Meditation is a simple relaxation technique that can be done almost anywhere.

alternative asthma treatments include certain techniques.

The Buteyko method, the Papworth method, and yoga all introduce breathing techniques that may reduce your need for medication. Meditation, biofeedback, hypnosis, and progressive muscle relaxation are relaxation techniques that can reduce stress and relieve asthma symptoms. Some people suffering from asthma have turned to herbal remedies, but herbs should be taken only under your health-care provider's supervision. Lastly, a change in your diet may help alleviate asthma symptoms. A diet rich in omega-3 fatty acids, or anti-inflammatory nutrients, may reduce chronic inflammation in your lungs. Foods rich in omega-3 fats are fish and flaxseed.

LIFESTYLE

If you have asthma, there's a fair chance you'll need some sort of medication to help you manage your condition. But medication is just one component of treating asthma. Your lifestyle is just as important. There are many things you can do in your everyday life to reduce your risk of asthma attacks and stay in good health. When you make an effort to stay in overall good health, you also help control your asthma.

Berries, such as blackberries, blueberries, and strawberries, are rich sources of antioxidants.

There are a few ways you can do that. First, eat well. Fruits and vegetables, in particular, are loaded with antioxidants. These nutrients give your immune system a boost and may minimize your asthma symptoms. Exercise regularly. This can strengthen your lungs and heart, which helps reduce asthma symptoms. Before you start an exercise regimen, talk to your doctor. Find out if you should take any special precautions, such as using your inhaler 30 minutes before exercising or wearing a face mask when exercising outdoors. An inhaler is a small device that delivers medicine in the form of gas. Watch your weight. Being overweight is a risk factor for developing or aggravating asthma.

In addition, it is important to reduce your exposure to substances or conditions that trigger your asthma symptoms. There are many ways your family can reduce triggers in and around your home. Avoid pets with fur or feathers, which carry pet dander. Get serious about reducing dust, pollen, and other airborne irritants and allergens. You can do this by using dust-proof covers for pillows, mattresses, and box springs. Change your bedding often and wash sheets in hot water.

On a larger scale, talk to you parents about the possibility of installing a high-efficiency particulate air (HEPA) filter on your furnace, air conditioner, and vacuum cleaner. Vacuum or mop floors often using vinegar—not bleach or any other toxic cleaner. See if you can replace carpet with wood, tile, or vinyl flooring. Use washable fabric curtains or blinds, or replace them with wooden or metal window coverings. Try to clean your house at least once a week. Cleaning often can also help prevent mold. Keep damp areas, such as the bathroom, clean. Clear damp leaves or wood from your yard. Lastly, run

Pets that carry dander should either be kept outside or groomed and bathed regularly.

your air conditioner when it's warm enough to do so. Air conditioning allows you to close your windows during pollen season. It also lowers the humidity indoors, which can help keep the dust mite population down. A dehumidifier may help, too.

MONITORING SYMPTOMS AND MAKING A PLAN

Monitoring your symptoms can help you know how well your treatment is controlling your asthma. You could keep a journal of your medication use and symptoms, or you might use a peak-flow meter to track your lung function.

You should work with your doctor to create an asthma action plan. This plan describes when to take certain medications—and how much to take—based on your symptoms. It should also include a list of your triggers and what you must do to avoid them.

Whatever your asthma treatment involves, it should be flexible. If your pattern of symptoms or the severity of your condition changes, your treatment should change, too. For example, your current treatment may result in better control of your asthma and a dramatic reduction in symptoms. In this case, your health-care provider might decide you need less medication and change your treatment plan.

COMPLICATIONS OF ASTHMA

If you have asthma, you should keep it as controlled as possible. Control is important not only because it keeps you safe and makes your life more pleasant now, but also because it prevents future complications of asthma. A couple of the most serious long-term complications of asthma are pneumonia or airway remodeling.

In some people with asthma, long-term inflammation of the airways causes permanent changes in the lungs. Some of these changes can be thicker airway membranes, scar tissue in the airways, and enlarged airway muscles and mucus glands. These changes further narrow the airways, aggravate asthma symptoms, and lead to reduced lung function.

DEPRESSION

Depression is an emotional complication that can arise from dealing with asthma. If you feel extremely sad and hopeless for long periods of time, and learning more doesn't help you feel better, it's time to talk to someone about your feelings. Here are some signs you might be suffering from depression:

- Sleeping, eating, or drinking more often or less than normal
- Feeling restless, agitated, or anxious
- Feeling worthless or excessively guilty
- Having difficulty dealing with everyday situations
- Feeling unable to think or concentrate
- Losing interest in activities and relationships you once enjoyed
- Disliking yourself and neglecting your health and personal hygiene
- Having frequent thoughts of death or suicide
- Losing or gaining a significant amount of weight
- Abusing drugs and alcohol

If several of these signs apply to you, talk to someone about it. Confide in a parent, a friend, your doctor, school nurse, a teacher or coach, a pastor or youth leader, or anyone you trust. Sharing these feelings is the first step toward relieving them.

ASK YOURSELF THIS

- *If you have asthma or someone you know does, what steps must be taken every day to avoid triggers?*

- *What have you done around your home to help avoid your asthma triggers?*

- *Has your asthma, or that of someone you know, improved or gotten worse over time? Has the treatment changed? How?*

- *Have you tried alternative asthma therapies? What kind of effect did they have?*

COPING WITH ASTHMA

R osie was 15. She'd had asthma since she was ten. For four years, Rosie's asthma was no big deal. She did, more or less, what she liked. She still played soccer in the summer and skied in the winter. She rarely missed school. She hung out with friends on the weekends.

But throughout the past year, Rosie's asthma had been worsening. She was having more frequent and severe attacks. Exercise had become a major trigger. She found herself sitting out of many soccer games and other activities.

Rosie felt a mix of emotions. Her asthma had become unpredictable, which made her feel anxious. She worried every time she left her house. Meanwhile, she felt helpless and sad— and hopping mad—about her bad luck.

Rosie's parents had noticed the change in her mood. One day, when they heard her answer the phone and turn down an invitation to go biking with her friends, they decided to speak up.

"What's wrong, honey? Not feeling well today?" they asked.

"I'm fine," said Rosie. "I just don't want to go." She slumped into a chair.

"Rosie, it's not cold out. Your friends know not to push you too hard. Your asthma will be just fine. Even if you do have a flare-up, you know what to do."

"I just don't want to go," Rosie snapped.

Rosie's parents didn't badger her. But later they approached the problem from another angle.

"Rosie," her mom said, pointing to her computer screen, "I see that your allergy clinic offers an asthma support group for teens. Interested in checking it out?"

Rosie looked skeptical. "What good would that do?" she asked.

"Well," said her mom, "I know you're feeling pretty bummed about your asthma. And you're right: it is a stroke of bad luck. But you don't have to take this bad luck lying down. Would it help if you knew you weren't alone? Other teens who have asthma might give you some coping ideas that would never occur to your dad and me."

It took some persuasion, but eventually Rosie went to a meeting. And then she went to another and another. She began to feel less isolated and more empowered, and both her mood and her health improved.

RELATIONSHIPS

Since asthma affects your daily life, it's bound to affect your relationships with other people. Sometimes having asthma can make it harder to deal with your family and friends. Your parents love you. It's their responsibility to keep you safe, healthy, and happy. They take that

Keep friends close and help them understand your condition.

responsibility seriously. And they're very used to taking care of you. After all, they've been doing it since you were a baby. But you're a teenager now. You may not want your parents hovering over you and telling you what to do all the time—nagging you to take your meds, making sure you have your inhaler with you, and so on. They might be getting on your nerves. You want to make your own decisions. You might be tempted to leave your inhaler at home, just to show them who's in charge.

Before you do that, you might want to stop and think about a couple of things. First, your parents aren't actually trying to annoy you; they just want to keep you safe. Second, you might have better luck getting them to back off if you show them responsibility instead of defiance. Chances are, defiance will just make them hover and nag even more.

When you're a teenager, life is more pleasant when you fit in. Unfortunately, having asthma can make you stick out like a sore thumb. Perhaps you need to take your meds at school. Or maybe there are some activities you just can't join your friends in doing. Some kids might tease you, calling you a wimp. First of all, realize friends who tease you aren't very good friends. If that's happening to you, you might want to call them out on their behavior—and if it doesn't change, find some better friends to spend time with.

Good friends won't treat you any differently just because you have asthma. They probably want to understand your condition better and know how to help if it flares up. You can just tell them directly about your triggers, your symptoms, and your action plan. And then you can all move on to more interesting things.

EMOTIONS

You've already learned emotions can affect asthma. It probably won't surprise you to learn the reverse is true, too. Although asthma is a physical illness, it is bound to affect your emotions. Having asthma can be stressful—and a little scary. If you've ever had a severe attack, you might worry about if or when you'll have another one. Maybe you've heard of people dying from asthma. You know it doesn't happen often, but it does happen.

Asthma is a serious disease, but there are ways to prepare. If you're scared, the best thing you can do is make sure you have an action plan for every scenario—and then follow it. Plan for mistakes. For example, keep several quick-relief inhalers in different places: one at home, one in your school locker, one in your backpack, one in your soccer bag, and so on. That way, you'll be ready for anything.

PANIC ATTACKS

Researchers at the National Institute of Mental Health have found that people who have asthma suffer from frequent panic attacks. Panic attacks are sudden feelings of terror that strike without warning and often without reason. In a 2005 study, researchers found the risk of developing panic disorder, a condition involving repeated, unexplained panic attacks, was nearly five times greater in people with asthma than in others. And people with panic disorder were approximately six times more likely to develop asthma within the following 20 years.[1]

ASTHMA SUPPORT GROUPS

Because of your asthma, you may sometimes feel sad about your current situation or uncertain about the future. These feelings are normal. It's

The best place to start looking for an asthma support group is at your own clinic.

okay to feel them, but do try to relieve them, too. You can often lighten such feelings by learning what asthma is and how to control it. Knowing more can help you feel empowered instead of helpless.

The people around you are your best sources of everyday support. Family, friends, teachers, and coaches can help you just by understanding your condition, accepting you, and knowing what to do in case you have an asthma attack.

It's also nice to get support from people who know exactly what it's like to be a teen with asthma: other teens with asthma. If your school or clinic doesn't offer an asthma support group for teens, check with your health insurance company.

ASK YOURSELF THIS

- *Have you or a friend been teased because of asthma? What was said? How did you or your friend respond?*

- *Do you ever feel afraid for yourself or a loved one with asthma? What are you afraid of, specifically? How could you relieve that fear?*

- *Can you identify one or more friends or adults with whom you can talk to about your asthma-related feelings?*

- *If you have asthma, what have you told your friends about it?*

ASTHMA CAMP

Maybe you've opted out of summer camp because your condition is too severe, your medication needs are too complex, or your family isn't convinced you'll be safe away from home. Asthma camp is a regular camp, but it's only for those with persistent asthma. Asthma camps are staffed by highly trained medical professionals. Asthma camps allow kids and teens with asthma to connect with peers, have fun, get away from home, and experience the outdoors in a medically safe way. To find a camp near you, visit http://www.asthmacamps.org/findacamp.cfm.

REACHING OUT

Sam's best friend was Corey. They'd met a few years ago when they started attending the same school and both joined the swim team.

Corey had asthma. But Sam didn't know. Corey hadn't said a word about it. Corey was a fast swimmer and worked hard at practices. Sam never would've guessed that Corey had a breathing problem.

Sam found out when Corey had an attack in the pool one day. He stopped in the middle of a drill, wheezing loudly. Coach Hamm asked Corey if he was okay. Corey couldn't answer, so Mr. Hamm dropped his clipboard and jumped into the pool. He pulled Corey to the edge, shouting, "Call 911!"

Sam was confused. He stopped by Corey's house the next day, after Corey came home from the hospital. "All right," he demanded. "What was that all about?"

Corey looked sheepish. "I have asthma," he said. "I keep an inhaler in my backpack. I'm supposed to take a puff 30 minutes before swim practice. I did take a puff yesterday—but my inhaler ran out. I didn't want to skip practice or make a big stink about it. Mr. Hamm knows I have asthma; if I told him, he would've benched me. So I just swam."

"Jeez," said Sam. "First of all: do you have a death wish or something? And second: why didn't you ever say anything about your asthma?"

"I don't want everyone thinking I'm an invalid," answered Corey.

SWIMMING AND ASTHMA

Swimming is an excellent form of exercise, especially if you have asthma. Because swimmers breathe air that's next to the water's surface, which means it is warmer and moister than ordinary air, swimming is less likely to cause asthma symptoms. Also, in addition to promoting overall fitness, swimming helps develop good breathing techniques and increase lung volume.

If you're worried about chlorine, know that research shows chlorine is only likely to be problematic if you're swimming in an indoor pool not properly ventilated. In fact, a 2011 to 2012 review of studies showed swimming improved lung function with no harmful effects on asthma control.[1]

"But what if Coach Hamm hadn't been right there?" said Sam. "He's the only one who knew, right?"

"Uh . . . yeah. Good point. But . . . I don't like being a freak. Or dragging down everyone's fun."

"Look, Corey. Everybody's got some kind of problem. Asthma isn't any weirder than any other problem. It makes no difference to me—or anyone else. We'd rather know how to help you," said Sam. "And don't worry, we won't treat you like an invalid. You're not *that* special." He grinned. Corey laughed and nodded. "Okay," he said.

PROVIDING EVERYDAY SUPPORT

Since nearly 10 percent of children in the United States have asthma, chances are good that if you don't have asthma yourself, you know someone who does.[2] If you have friends or family members with asthma, you might wonder if there's anything you can do to help them. You can do a lot, both psychologically and physically. Here are some ideas for emotionally supporting someone with asthma:

- Be encouraging. Focus on what the person can do instead of what he or she can't. Acknowledge the difficult situation and congratulate the person for coping with it.

- Bring laughter. If you know the person well, make jokes and do things he or she will find funny.

- Check in often, even if it's just to let the person know he or she is in your thoughts. Keep an eye on the person's emotional state.

- Don't treat your friend or relative as an outcast. Remember he or she is a person, not an asthma case.

- Go along to support group meetings. These offer great opportunities to learn more and ask questions.

- If you don't know what to say, just admit it and say, "I'm here for you." And then keep your word and be present.

Learn about asthma. Research on your own and ask questions to show your friend or family member you're interested.

- Make it clear you're always available to listen. Then follow up on your promise and listen whenever your friend or relative wants to talk.

- Offer specific help. For example: "Do you want me to bring your schoolwork home?" or "Do you need anything at the store?"

You can help your friend or family member physically, too. Learn as much as you can about the person's specific triggers and symptoms. Know where he or she keeps quick-relief inhalers. Learn the names of all your friend's or relative's medications, what they are used for, and when. And finally, know what to do in an emergency.

HELPING IN AN EMERGENCY

Your friend or relative may have an asthma attack while spending time with you. If you're prepared for that possibility, you can be a big help. If you find yourself in this situation, be calm and reassuring. Panic can make breathing even harder, so help the person relax. Next, get the person away from asthma triggers and keep the person upright. Lying down can make

WHAT NOT TO DO

- Don't tell the person how he or she should feel.
- Don't compare the person to someone else.
- Don't discuss worst-case scenarios unless the person brings it up. If he or she does want to talk about scary possibilities, don't shy away. Remember this is really hard for your friend or relative.
- Don't give medical advice. Chances are, you aren't qualified to do so, and this should be left to your friend or relative's doctor.
- Don't downplay the person's condition or criticize him or her for complaining.
- Don't suggest activities you know the person can't do.

If you think a friend with asthma may start panicking, try your best to calm him or her down.

breathing more difficult. Ask the person what should be done during an asthma attack. If he or she can tell you, follow the action plan. Get the person's quick-relief inhaler and help him or her use it. If the inhaler isn't working, the person can't talk, his or her lips or fingernails start to turn color, or the person passes out, call 911 immediately.

ASK YOURSELF THIS

- *If you have a friend with asthma, did he or she keep it quiet at first? Why?*

- *What questions would you like to ask your friend or relative with asthma?*

- *What could you say to your friend or relative with asthma to inspire a smile?*

- *Do you know your friend or relative's asthma triggers, symptoms, and medications? What are they?*

- *Have you ever helped someone having an asthma attack? What did you do? Were you scared?*

CALLING 911

If you're not sure whether you should call 911, call. The dispatcher can decide whether your situation is an emergency and what type of help to send. When you call 911, be prepared to give the following information:

- Where you are, including the street address
- The number of the phone you are calling from
- What the emergency is (an asthma attack)
- Details about the emergency, such as the symptoms of the person having an asthma attack
- Follow any instructions the dispatcher gives you.
- Don't hang up until the dispatcher tells you to.

LOOKING FORWARD

Nineteen-year-old Liv has had asthma for almost ten years. When she was younger, her symptoms were pretty bad. Looking back, Liv could see it was because she didn't understand asthma very well. Back then, she was still trying to figure out what her

Asthma is manageable and shouldn't hold you back from enjoying life as a teen.

triggers were. Since she didn't really know what was causing her symptoms, she couldn't avoid the culprits. Also, at first she wasn't very good at recognizing the early signs of an asthma attack. So she'd be in full-blown wheeze mode before she realized she needed to take action.

Now, Liv was an expert. She knew she was allergic to dogs, cats, and a bunch of different tree pollens. She simply avoided dogs and cats. And she took her allergy meds religiously in the springtime. With her allergies under control, her asthma rarely flared up. Even when it did, Liv could feel an attack coming on in plenty of time to head it off.

At Liv's yearly checkup, her health-care provider congratulated her. "You've really come a long way, young lady." Dr. Jansen smiled and showed her a chart of her lung function over the years. "Your lung function is nearly normal now, because you take such good care of yourself. Well done!"

Liv patted herself on the back for wising up about asthma. She was doing really well health-wise—much better than ten years ago. But sometimes Liv worried about the future. She wondered if those early years of poor control and severe attacks had done damage to her lungs.

Only time would tell. So Liv tried not to dwell on it. She knew she couldn't change the past. And she knew how to take good care of herself now. Taking good care of herself was the best path to breathing easily in her old age.

ASTHMA INTO ADULTHOOD

If you're a teen with asthma, you might want to consider adopting Liv's attitude. The better you take care of yourself now, the better health you can expect as you move through adulthood.

Recent research conducted by the Yale School of Public Health suggests taking care of your asthma symptoms when you are young can have lasting impacts. Researchers found that children with asthma have a 12 percent higher risk of adult obesity. Reasons for this could be habits from childhood, such as not engaging in exercise, in an attempt to avoid asthma attacks. The study also found that young adults

FAMOUS PEOPLE WITH ASTHMA

Even if you end up having lifelong asthma, it shouldn't prevent you from achieving your goals. Many high-profile leaders, artists, and athletes had—or have—asthma. Did you know football stars Jerome Bettis and Emmitt Smith have asthma? How about rocker Alice Cooper and actor Sharon Stone? Beloved fiction writer Charles Dickens had asthma, too. And so did past presidents and other leaders, such as Theodore Roosevelt and John F. Kennedy. For more asthma heroes, see http://www.getasthmahelp.org/famous-people.aspx.

who suffered from childhood asthma had up to 50 percent more absenteeism from school and work.[1]

HOW LONG WILL ASTHMA LAST?

If you have asthma now, you may wonder if you'll always have it. A longitudinal study of 868 children in New Zealand offers some insight. In this study, researchers used frequent questionnaires, allergy screenings, and breathing tests to see which kids got asthma. By age 15, approximately 20 percent of the whole group had asthma. Of those kids, 40 percent said their asthma was gone by the time they turned 18. But eight years later, many of those 68 had asthma again. Asthma returned in 24 kids by age 26. That's approximately 35 percent of the people whose asthma had gone away.[2]

In other words: you can control asthma. But you have to take care of your health in order to give yourself the best chance of taking control. Avoid behaviors, conditions, and substances that raise your risk of asthma, such as smoking,

FACTORS IN OUTGROWING ASTHMA

If you have asthma now, you're more likely to have asthma through adulthood if:

- You had persistent wheezing during early childhood.
- You have a skin allergy such as eczema or you have hay fever.
- You have severe asthma.

Take control of your asthma to live your life doing the things you love!

obesity, secondhand smoke, allergens, and jobs that expose you to chemical irritants. See your health provider, take your medication, educate yourself about your symptoms and controlling them, and reduce triggers in your environment.

ASK YOURSELF THIS

- *How have you gotten better at managing your asthma over time?*

- *In what ways might you do a better job than you're doing now?*

- *Do you think your asthma will go away or persist? Why?*

- *Do you know any adults who used to have asthma but don't anymore?*

- *Do you know any adults who have had asthma since they were children?*

JUST THE FACTS

Asthma is a chronic lung disease with a key characteristic of inflammation of the airways. This inflammation leads to environmental reactions that narrow the airways.

The symptoms of asthma vary from person to person—and from episode to episode—in type, intensity, duration, and frequency. However, four key symptoms appear in most people with asthma at some point. These symptoms are wheezing, coughing, chest discomfort, and shortness of breath.

An asthma trigger is a condition or substance that causes asthma symptoms to either start or get worse. Categories of triggers include irritants, allergens, drugs, emotional behaviors, exercise, infections, and weather.

Asthma is an immunological disorder in which the body overreacts to perceived—but not actual—dangers. When a combination of genetic and environmental factors meet, usually in childhood, a person may develop asthma. The causal factors may include inherited allergies, having parents with asthma, having certain respiratory infections as a child, and having been exposed to certain allergens, irritants, or viruses in early childhood.

Risk factors for asthma include gender, family history, having another allergic condition, exposure to smoking, exposure to air pollution, and being overweight.

Asthma complications include symptoms that interfere with sleep, work, or recreational activities; permanent narrowing of the bronchial tubes (airway remodeling); and side effects from long-term use of some medications.

The process of determining whether a person has asthma includes documenting a detailed personal and family medical history; completing a physical examination of the airways and the skin; and performing tests such as spirometry, allergy blood and skin testing, bronchoprovocation, and a chest X-ray.

An asthma diagnosis includes a severity grade. Grading indicates physical condition, lung function, and the frequency and severity of symptoms. Grades include intermittent asthma, mild persistent asthma, moderate persistent asthma, and severe persistent asthma.

Coping methods for asthma sufferers include learning about asthma, keeping it under control, being prepared, and finding support from friends, family, and other trusted people.

The best ways to support a person with asthma are to be present, to learn about asthma, and to know what to do in an emergency.

WHERE TO TURN

If You Want to Clear Your Home of Asthma Triggers

There are many things you can do to change your environment, reduce your risk of asthma attacks, and stay in good health. Avoid pets with fur or feathers, or regularly bathe and groom your pets if they are in the home. Reduce dust, pollen, and other airborne irritants and allergens by using dust-proof covers in your bedroom, cleaning often, using HEPA filters, washing fabric items often, and running the air conditioner instead of opening windows. Keep damp areas clean, use a dehumidifier, and keep the yard free of wet leaves and wood to prevent mold.

If Someone Has an Asthma Attack While in Your Company

First of all, be calm and reassuring. Help the person relax to try and get his or her breathing under control. Get the person away from asthma triggers, and keep the person upright. Lying down can make breathing more difficult. If you're not already sure what to do, ask the person. If he or she can tell you, follow the action plan. Get the person's quick-relief inhaler and help him or her use it. Call 911 if the person can't talk or is struggling to breathe, if the inhaler doesn't help, if an inhaler isn't available, if the person's lips or fingernails turn bluish or grayish, or if the person passes out.

If Your Family Is Struggling with the Financial Cost of Asthma

Asthma medications and treatment can be very expensive, but there are resources available to help. Visit the Asthma and Allergy Foundation of America Web site with your parents: http://www.aafa.org/display.cfm?id=5&sub=105&cont=677 This resource lists multiple programs that may be helpful if your family is finding it difficult to cover the costs of asthma.

If You Want to Know More about Air Quality in Your Area

Controlling your asthma requires education. It's important to be educated about your surroundings. If you plan to be outdoors, be knowledgeable about the air quality in your area to see if outdoor activities are a healthy choice for you. You can find your local AQI or download a free AQI smartphone app at http://airnow.gov.

GLOSSARY

air quality index (AQI)
A measure of five major air pollutants.

airway
A passage that carries air from outside the body to the inside of the body.

allergen
Any substance that causes an allergic reaction.

alveolus
A tiny round air sac at the end of the bronchioles, where oxygen enters the blood and carbon dioxide exits the blood.

bronchiole
A smaller airway inside the lungs that branches off the bronchi.

bronchus
A tube that branches off the lower end of the trachea and leads into the lungs.

Buteyko method
An alternative form of asthma treatment that uses shallow breathing and breath-holding techniques to help manage asthma.

capillary
A tiny blood vessel.

eosinophil
A white blood cell involved in allergic reactions.

inflammation
The body's natural response to illness, injury, pain, or stress. Blood, antibodies, and other immune substances rush in to break down damaged tissue, kill germs, and rebuild healthy tissue, causing swelling, redness, heat, pain, and/or loss of function.

longitudinal study
A research method in which data is repeatedly observed and gathered about the same subjects over a period of time.

Papworth method
An alternative form of asthma treatment that uses shallow breathing and relaxation exercises to help manage asthma.

prognosis
The outlook of recovery for a disease.

trachea
A tube that leads from the nose and mouth to the lungs.

trigger
A condition or substance that causes asthma symptoms to either start or get worse.

ADDITIONAL RESOURCES

SELECTED BIBLIOGRAPHY

Adams, Francis V. *The Asthma Sourcebook*. New York: McGraw-Hill, 2007. Print.

Plottel, Claudia S. *100 Questions and Answers about Asthma*. Sudbury, MA: Jones and Bartlett, 2011. Print.

Simmons, Janice C. *The Everything Parent's Guide to Children with Asthma*. Avon, MA: Adams, 2008. Print.

Welch, Michael J. *Allergies and Asthma: What Every Parent Needs to Know*. Elk Grove Village, IL: American Academy of Pediatrics, 2011. Print.

FURTHER READINGS

Paquette, Penny Hutchins. *Asthma: The Ultimate Teen Guide*. Lanham, MD: Scarecrow, 2006. Print.

Sheen, Barbara. *Asthma*. Detroit: Lucent, 2011. Print.

Wohlenhaus, Kim. *Asthma Information for Teens*. Detroit: Omnigraphics, 2009. Print.

WEB SITES

To learn more about living with asthma, visit ABDO Publishing Company online at **www.abdopublishing.com**. Web sites about living with asthma are featured on our Book Links page. These links are routinely monitored and updated to provide the most current information available.

SOURCE NOTES

CHAPTER 1. WHAT IS ASTHMA?

1. "Asthma Surveillance Data." *CDC.gov*. Centers for Disease Control and Prevention, 25 Mar. 2013. Web. 1 May 2013.

CHAPTER 2. ASTHMA SYMPTOMS

1. "That Nagging Cough." *Harvard Health Publications*. Harvard University, Sept. 2010. Web. 3 July 2013.

CHAPTER 3. THE CAUSES OF ASTHMA

1. "Hygiene Hypothesis." *PBS.org*. WGBH Educational Foundation, 2001. Web. 17 May 2013.

2. Francis V. Adams. *The Asthma Sourcebook*. New York: McGraw-Hill, 2007. 184. Print.

3. Jane E. Brody. "A Breathing Technique Offers Help for People with Asthma." *New York Times*. New York Times, 2 Nov. 2009. Web. 17 May 2013.

4. "Today's AQI Forecast." *AirNow.gov*. US Environmental Protection Agency, 2013. Web. 18 May 2013.

CHAPTER 4. WHO'S AT RISK FOR ASTHMA?

1. Padmaja Subbarao, et al. "Asthma: Epidemiology, Etiology, and Risk Factors." *Canadian Medical Association Journal*. Canadian Medical Association, 27 Oct. 2009. Web. 5 June 2013.

2. C. Almqvist. "Impact of Gender on Asthma in Childhood and Adolescence: A GA2LEN Review." *PubMed.gov*. US National Library of Medicine, Jan. 2008. Web. 4 July 2013.

3. Padmaja Subbarao, et al. "Asthma: Epidemiology, Etiology, and Risk Factors." *Canadian Medical Association Journal*. Canadian Medical Association, 27 Oct. 2009. Web. 5 June 2013.

4. Jenny Marder. "Air Pollution Boosts a Child's Chance of Getting Cockroach-Related Asthma." *PBS NewsHour.* MacNeil/Lehrer Productions, 6 Feb. 2013. Web. 5 June 2013.

5. Ibid.

6. Padmaja Subbarao, et al. "Asthma: Epidemiology, Etiology, and Risk Factors." *Canadian Medical Association Journal.* Canadian Medical Association, 27 Oct. 2009. Web. 5 June 2013.

7. "Asthma and Air Pollution." *California Environmental Protection Agency Air Resources Board.* Air Resources Board, 5 Feb. 2013. Web. 5 June 2013.

8. Padmaja Subbarao, et al. "Asthma: Epidemiology, Etiology, and Risk Factors." *Canadian Medical Association Journal.* Canadian Medical Association, 27 Oct. 2009. Web. 5 June 2013.

9. "Why Obese People Have Higher Rates of Asthma." *ScienceDaily.* ScienceDaily, 8 Jan. 2013. Web. 6 July 2013.

10. "US Asthma Rates Continue to Rise." *CDC.gov.* Centers for Disease Control and Prevention, 11 May 2011. Web. 5 June 2013.

CHAPTER 5. GETTING AN ASTHMA DIAGNOSIS

1. "Mild, Moderate, Severe Asthma: What Do Grades Mean?" *Healthychildren.org.* American Academy of Pediatrics, 11 May 2013. Web. 7 June 2013.

2. Ibid.

3. Ibid.

SOURCE NOTES CONTINUED

CHAPTER 6. TREATING ASTHMA AND PREVENTING ATTACKS

1. "Asthma History—Through the Ages." *Medical News Today*. MediLexicon, 2013. Web. 7 June 2013.

CHAPTER 7. COPING WITH ASTHMA

1. Gregor Hasler, et al. "Asthma and Panic in Young Adults: A 20-Year Prospective Community Study." *PubMed.gov*. US National Library of Medicine, 1 June 2005. Web. 8 June 2013.

CHAPTER 8. REACHING OUT

1. Sean Beggs, et al. "Swimming Training for Asthma in Children and Adolescents Aged 18 Years and Under." *The Cochrane Library*. John Wiley & Sons, 30 Apr. 2013. Web. 9 June 2013.

2. "Asthma Surveillance Data." *CDC.gov*. Centers for Disease Control and Prevention, 25 Mar. 2013. Web. 9 June 2013.

CHAPTER 9. LOOKING FORWARD

1. "Childhood Asthma Found to Negatively Affect Adult Health." *Yale News*. Yale University, 6 May 2010. Web. 10 June 2013.

2. Miranda Hitti. "Who's At Risk for Asthma Relapse?" *WebMD*. WebMD, 7 Mar. 2005. Web. 10 Jun. 2013.

INDEX

ABOUT THE AUTHOR

Christine Zuchora-Walske has been writing and editing books and articles for children, parents, and teachers for more than 20 years. Her author credits include books for children and young adults on science, history, and current events; books for adults on pregnancy and parenting; and more. Her book *Giant Octopuses* was an IRA Teacher's Choice book for 2001, and *Leaping Grasshoppers* was a 2001 NSTA/CBC Outstanding Science Trade Book for Students. Several of Zuchora-Walske's books have been well reviewed by *Horn Book* and *School Library Journal*. Zuchora-Walske lives in Minneapolis, Minnesota, with her husband and two children.